THE

Badass Babe

COLORING BOOK

*This book is dedicated to
Badass Babes and Cosmocat Colorists.*

*Thank you for the colorful rainbow of cosmic
badassery that only you bring to life in the world.*

· · · ———————— ♡ ———————— · · ·

FIRST EDITION

PUBLISHED 2017 BY COSMOCAT™

· ·

SHARE YOUR COLORING WORK ON INSTAGRAM!
TAG AND LINK @COSMOCAT_BOOKS

+

VISIT **COSMOCATBOOKS.COM** AND REGISTER WITH
YOUR EMAIL TO RECEIVE YOUR FREE DOWNLOAD COPY
OF THE BADASS BABE MANIFESTO ⟶

THE
Badass Babe
MANIFESTO

I AM WILD
I AM FREE
THERE IS NOBODY JUST LIKE ME

I AM AUTHENTIC
I AM TRUE
THERE IS NOTHING I CANNOT DO

I AM COURAGEOUS
I AM STRONG
I SHOW THE WORLD MY INNER SONG

I AM PASSIONATE
I AM LIT
I RISE UP AFTER TAKING A HIT

I FACE MY SHADOWS
I BRING THEM TO LIGHT
I INVITE GRACE TO MAKE THINGS RIGHT

I DREAM BIG
AND FOLLOW MY HEART
MY LIFE IS MY WORK OF ART

I LOVE MYSELF EVERY DAY
I KNOW MY BEAUTY IN EVERY WAY

HEART. MIND. BODY & SOUL
I SEE MY SHIMMERING RAINBOW

I AM A BADASS BABE

LIVING THE ADVENTURE
LAUGHING ON THE GO

DANCING AND DARING
INTO THE MAGIC UNKNOWN

This coloring book
belongs to

_____

A Badass Babe

Badass

Coloring

Test

Page

OPTIONAL: CUT THIS PAGE OUT AND PLACE
BEHIND ARTWORK FOR BLEED-THROUGH PROTECTION

My Beautiful Badassery

Moon Dancer